Strength, labour and sorrow

Poems and other writings by

KERRY WHITE

celebrating 70 years

Self-published.

2015©

ISBN 978-0-9942814-1-8

(Revised edition)

Previously by the author: *the poet from hell*, 2013

Published by CreateSpace Independent Publishing Platform

(ISBN: 978-1491031278 or 1491031271)

Both available through Amazon and other online booksellers

as well as in Kindle.

> *The days of our years are threescore years and ten;*
>
> *and if by reason of strength they be fourscore years,*
>
> *yet is their strength labour and sorrow;*
>
> *for it is soon cut off, and we fly away.*
>
> *– Moses, Psalm 90:10*

PREFACE

The words opposite seem appropriate since I am turning 70, though I hope to take advantage of increased life expectancy since they were written. Even 70 must have been a good innings then. I have used the words in the book title in a positive sense: strength in life from good things; 'labour' the work one has put in both career-wise and otherwise, and the 'sorrow' in life we deal with and hopefully move on. One might hope for a few more years before life is 'cut off' and I 'fly away'.

My first book published in November 2013 seemed to have some readers a little concerned with its title of *the poet from hell*, a reference to a saying from the Vietnam War: "When I die I'll go to heaven 'cause I've spent my time in hell". Anyway, to quote Dante's Inferno Canto XXXIV: 70-139: "The Poets leave Hell. And again behold the stars".

Thanks to all those who supported me in my first book venture. This book includes both poetry and non-fiction prose. It is dedicated to all who have been kind enough to be my mate, friend, brother, sister, lover, colleague, boss … but particularly to my mother who gave even more than a mother might be expected to give, and to my sons, Nicholas and Patrick *(they are pictured a few years ago outside the family home in Toowoomba).*

Hope the read is enjoyable and worthwhile.

Best wishes always.

Kerry White

'*A son of the Darling Downs*'

Typical Darling Downs scene: cover photo by the author's niece, Helen Nolan.

CONTENTS

Seventy years … still going	1
Ever ever land	7
Growing older now	8
A swig in the park	10
Anniversary for those who have flown	11
Another year AD	12
Clock windeth back	13
Boxing Day	14
Place of memory	15
What day is it?	16
Laugh and pain	17
Penguins on ice	18
Not any war	19
Sands of time	20
Played the dream	21
Slipping memories	22
Tale of two oceans	23
Time is …	24
Status update	25
Water gliding	26
Pray tell	27
Yuletide time	28
Scenario	29
Poll of omens	30
For Australia's Day	31
What may be	32
Murder on the nile express	33
Arabian nights	34
Elegy in a country churchyard	35
Other writings:	
Reflections on newspapers	40
An amazing month on the other side	43
Family link ends after 100 years	51
Churches big and small	53
Time of learning and adventure	56
From little things …	60
Apprentice who became a hero	62

Seventy years on ... still going

A war about to end, wasn't to know,
Final tinkering with The Bomb,
Weeks after Dresden forced a hand
Counting down to a time of peace.
Born March 5 1945, far away
It's Oriental Year of the Rooster.
Remember coming home from hospital?
Not really, can imagine the welcome
From Dad, brother and three sisters.
Mother went through much apparently,
Sometimes a crabby housekeeper
Came from QCWA, icon of the bush,
Much more than cakes and biscuits,
Knitting, crocheting and gossip.
Once I walked out on said lady
Maybe missing a mother's love
As she was away in hospital,
Twilight came and went, no sign
Of an errant boy somewhere alone,
But just on dark maybe sensing alarm
He came out from behind the piano
Greeted by mixed emotions and
Out of tune with reality – maybe
That is why he didn't learn to play
Though music was in his soul –
Metaphoring future life.

Small town with two streets names
Obvious and plain – Main and Side.
Local Anzacs' names might have been
Remembered there stead of plaques
On pine trees by the school gate.
First memory is of church, the Mass
In a language he didn't know
Until boarding school much later:

In nomine Patris et fillii et Spiritus Sancti.
Memory first or second, Good Friday
Fishing by the willowed creek
Fish are fish, probably perch,
Didn't seem to matter then that
Dad put the fish on the hook
And he reeled it in – prize catch
As the child took the bait.
Then back home for Sunday best
On Good Friday, praying sadly for
Stations of the Cross – passion
Seemed malpropriate he thought
As an older thoughtful youth.

First day at school a rebel
Kicked teacher in the shins
Resisted education then for years
Always seemed to end in tears
Loved little lunch, lunch footy,
Back to copy book and blots,
Can't wait for the day to end.
In the playground hard and dry,
Bindi-eyes were all that grew
But barefoot kids were tough
And sometimes even rough
Though boys became so shy
When folk-dancing class
Meant touching blushing girls.
But life went on, holidays
Most special of times
Sometimes in father's store
Or in delivery trucks
For groceries, grain and fuel,
Or riding on tractors,
Bareback on friends' horses.
City trip for presents
Longer drive to the coast,
Sand, surf, fish and chips.

Rain came, rushing brown torrents
Filled streets and paddocks
Making play dams in town gutters
Bogged in sticky black soil.
Cats and rats, mice and elephants
Reality and dreams confuse,
Show me yours I'll show you mine,
Taught that God knew all of
Everything done or even thought
Meant fear not so much of God
But of the man he had to tell
At the dreaded confessional.
Confiteor Deo omnipotenti.
Dressed in his Sunday best
He and other duly blessed
To take bread and eat it
First time at Communion.
Dominus vobiscum.
Novice faith sorely tested
The night his father died
Three boys in suits stand
Solemnly by a palm tree
As Dad is laid to rest
Much before his time.
A few years lost, times
Blurred with young tears,
Flowing over the years.
So boarding school was like
A prison for a while,
Regimented life of three Rs
With prayer and adoration,
Or the day the music died.
On the fields he found fun
Relief from class boredom
Wanting to be back in the bush
Where quietness could be found.
Somehow passed to move
To senior years, matured

*'Three boys ...
as Dad is laid
to rest.'*

Out of shyness king-hitting
A class bully to make a mark.
Will's merchants, history's wars,
Bewildering equations and
Logic somehow his best.
Holidays put all that behind,
Fun down on the farm,
Tractors, horses, driving,
Flirting moments at dances.
Back to footy and cricket,
No champ but having fun,
Smoking was his hazard
Almost had him leaving.

After school tractor-driving,
Instead of a paddock though
Round and round in a bank;
Rugby and its sideshows
Kept him off the streets.
Young town intellectuals
Also made for fun and talk,
Shock from a shot in Dallas.
Memories of war fed fears
Of invading hoards, peace
Has a price, birthday ballot
The answer for the threat.
So his number was up,
Celebrate his twenty-first
Learning to hide and kill
In the Adelaide Hills.
Off he went to conflict,
A country far away
Stained by centuries of war.
While young Diggers etched
Names on plaques or history
On a highway to hell
Home fires were burning
And blowing in the wind.
Back home they came
Greeted by thousands
Opposites in emotion, then
Goodbye and forgotten,
Memory canned for another day.
Unsettled like them all
Found work where he could
Newspapers got him in:
Note, type, sub, lead,
Print a daily miracle.
Romance settled him,
Love was in the air,
Mother to a son and heir
Another was to come along.

Different places, many faces,
Made a name in print
Drawing a fine line
News fair and fore.
Celebrate a Bicentennial
Mixed emotions for some
Festivity for others
Brisbane exposed for
A second coming of age.
In Canberra apolitical for
Memorial to the war so
Many sought to forget.

His resume changed
Again from government
To aged and chopper care.
Generations came to realise
Preciousness of mothers
And other special people
Gone before you're ready.
A special person inspired
Him to higher study
Achieving a distinct degree
That once was so cursory.
Children of another age
Gave cause for wonderment
Month by month actions,
Words in happy evolution.
Now by the ocean – nature
At its most supreme
Pausing, reflecting now and then
Reaching three score years and ten.

(Family lore has our old Mount Tyson home in Side Street, but today's GoogleMaps have it as Knust Road).

Ever ever land

We're not really racist, just
Worried about Our Land.
A big country, land down under,
But farmers big time going bellyup;
Generations ago they came here
To explore and make a new breed
A place they lived and breathed,
In some ways they felt the sacred
Spirit that was essence of the land
Like a snake, a serpent.
At times they would dream
Of a future bright and well
Where work brought reward,
Sheep shorn, cattle cut, grain grew,
Where the land gave opportunity
To those who battled on
Though many were lost to war
And others to the big smoke;
Still they soldiered on
Contributing to national wealth
Until a ship called Free Trade
And for reasons other − change
Came and it was never to be
The same in Never Never Land.
Old mate sitting on a bench
With a countenance of centuries
Says 'yeah mate, we had that
Problem too ...'

Growing older now

Growing older now
Like those they followed
Fathers and grandfathers
Nurses there to tender
Blooded in the veldt
Drenched at Gallipoli
Didn't end all wars
As another arose
Threats spanning oceans
Till blasts from the sky
Brought peace yet again
But not long until fire
Flared again to the north.

Growing older now
The tried and tested
Were ready for the fray
Where the legion failed
Cold war beliefs
Taking on an ideology
So people could be free
Training team became legend
When they blazed the path
Joined later by the first
Back home on birthdays
Celebrations dimmed
As teens were made men
Old heads and young heads
Became as one – mates
Looking after each other
Thinking they were right
Warriors day and night.

Growing older now
They read about the time

Photo of 7 RAR Diggers by Mike Coleridge – from Australian War Memorial Collection.

Their lives were on the line
When it all seemed so right
History turned the page
Answering to popular rage
So he and mates meet
Talking of tough times
Fun in other climes
While others in power
Moved on with their lives
These veterans remember.

ANZAC reputation intact
They won their battle
Not theirs the war.

- *For the fallen, fellow veterans and victims of the Vietnam War 1962-75.*
- *"The Australians were more patient than the Americans, better guerrilla fighters, better at ambushes. They liked to stay with us instead of calling in planes. We were more afraid of their style." – Trinh Duc, Xuan Loc District Branch Party Secretariat. NAM, The Vietnam Experience Vol. 13, p59.*
- *"We were all over Vietnam and I talked to a lot of people ... the only ones who knew how to fight this thing are the Australians and the Viet Cong. I sent company commanders to train with the Australians ... so they could pick up the skills of those well trained and careful jungle fighters." – Lt.Col. David Hackworth (a highly decorated United States veteran of World War Two, Korea and Vietnam) in* About Face.

A swig in the park

He loomed across the park,
From the hotel takeaway,
Just after opening
Plastic bag in hand,
Moulded by his hand
To make a bottle shape.
Walking intently, he sat
At the grey, stark bus stop.
Standing the bag almost ritually
While he rolled a durry.
He puffed and pondered
Maybe whether to open
What now obviously a bottle?
Was he thinking of his past
That got him where he is
Or his future, and the bottle,
To keep him where he is
Drowning memories.
He arose, walked slowly
Across the grass, under a tree,
Taking off shirt and jacket
All grubby like his skin,
Bedraggled hair grey atop
On his head, his beard and chest.
Jacket on the grass, bottle
Still in the bag, puffing away.
Is it time, yet, to begin the daily swill?

Anniversary: For those who have flown

Remember the gladness
Rather than sadness
Memories of good times
Better than sad times
Those wonderful moments
Among life's little torments
For we will all go where
Others are already there.

Photo by Helen Nolan, at her home, Inagh Park.

Another year AD

So agreed around
Our known world
That Anno Domini
Will have common
Universality - agreed then
It is now 2015.
Happy New Year!
Traditional enemies
Put aside hate
Formed over years,
Maybe centuries,
To agree the year
Is based on a belief
Not held by all
But understood.
Simple, no grouch
From non-believing
bureaucratic kings.
If such equanimity
Is so simple to achieve
Why the bloody hell
Is peace so difficult?

Clock windeth back

All the King's horses,
All the King's men,
Couldn't put the monarchy
Together again.
Down on bended knee
Dubbed with shades of yesteryear.
Currying favour in the Halls
Of power, corridors awash
With gushing praises for
Heroic giver of Royal Ascent.
Will all in ministrations
Around yon Cabinet bench
Be Knights – and Dames –
Of the oval table?
Except Malcom in the middle,
He doth protest, but 'Checkmate'
Interjects the Bishop
Who's to become a Dame:
'Don't step on the budgie'.
Chief Monk, finger to lips,
Reminds all sworn present
To keep it to themselves
Until official announcement date,
On April 1 they will be so dubbed.

- *Reintroduction of honours of Knights and Dames, March 2014.*

Boxing Day

Frantic, frenetic
Freespending
Frivolous
Saving dollars
Shoppers shuffle
Spin the plastic
Rush for bargains
Annual day for racing
To bulging shops
Or stay home
Clean the esky
Watch the cricket
Race for hobart
Or hit the beach
Life's a wave.

Place of memory

Chocolate, coffee
Never sweet again
Like yesterday
Children lose
A mother
A partner loses
A dear mate.
A memorial to
Our fallen
Stands nearby
In a place of peace
Shaken, stirred by
A different war.
Peace has left
This sacred place
Where I once stood guard
To the sombre echoes of
Lest We Forget.

Martin Place, Sydney – from City of Sydney website.

What day is it?

If tomorrow was yesterday
Would you do it different
Than if it were today?
If tomorrow was today
Would yesterday
Have been different?
If yesterday was today
Would it be better
To wait until tomorrow?
If today was tomorrow
Would yesterday
Be today, or today
Be tomorrow?

Laugh and pain

A land of contradictions,
A land of sleeping pains,
A land that roars with thunder,
When drought is sent asunder,
A land that's poor for rain
A land to drive you insane,
A land not suffered in vain
Where you can laugh and pain.

Such is the land of lore and legend
Land of ancients, blessed by time,
Rich past, symphony and sympathy,
Sweet present, with sour notes,
May future be of challenges won.

Penguins on ice

Reincarnated nuns,
A thousand penguins
March across the ice
Towards a fissure
Of fertility,
Family staying together
And preying together
In the end.
After the march to the altar
Of their procreation,
Reproduction on ice,
A scene of natural consummation,
Generated by holy orders,
Not allowed to take the habit
Of sweet human procreation,
Obvious as black and white.

*Micosoft
Clip Art*

Not any war

He'd been a hero of Milne Bay,
The battle that turned the war,
The real war, how he said it.
'Where were you?' he asked
Arrogantly, looking at the badge,
'Returned From Active Service'.
Didn't know there were any other
Possibilities, but 'Vietnam',
I said shyly, apologetically.
'That's not a war', he said,
As though it was just a backyard
Game of Cowboys and Indians.
He now Reserve Brigadier,
Me a Digger on leave from war.
'The bullets fly faster now', I said,
Walked away for another beer.
'I could be charged,' I thought.
Didn't see him again till years later,
Taking out his daughter, nothing
Was said about the war, any war.

Sands of time

Surf's up, boards out
Glide across the foam
Not alone, working hard
Ride it in ecstasy,
Hard work means
Going out again,
Teens loving life
Hair bleached,
Back on the sand
Dreaming
Tough to be born
In a lucky country
If you don't
Lose your head.
Half a world away
Teens same age
Part of a wave
Of new apostates
In the ancient sands
Of once proud
Civilisation schooled
In beheading in the name
Of a god that
Cannot exist:
If so return to
Evolution
And begin again
With peace essence
Of all souls.

Played the dream

Bush kid with a smile
He could stay for a while
Spreading the field,
Others in awe not envy,
As the blade unsheathed
His runs were plundered.
Leaving the family farm,
The city beckoned,
Not the bright lights,
But fields of green
Where he played the dream
Made the side of the nation,
Other times in frustration,
But always the smile
As he took the field,
His feet were planted
In his country roots
As he saw another chance
To continue the romance
Once more the Baggy Green
Still seems just a teen.
On 63, called by the Don,
And the smile has gone.

– *To Philip Hughes (photo newstribe.com)*

Slipping memories

Water licks the shore
Of the lake's sandy shore.
A long way from home
For a busload unknowing
Oblivious, or obvious,
Memories may be stirred
Of childhoods long ago
By other watery shores
When they were childlike,
Then late their children
Went to other sandy shores
As growing older, their children
Also found their own shores.
As tides come and go
Life has ups and downs
Till now a bus brings them
To this sandy shore.
Memories creak and stir
As they sip from a cup of tea
But all too soon
Restless they soon fret
Fearful of being left behind
Or of missing lunch back there.

– *Observing a busload of aged care patients visiting Lake Boreen.*

Tale of two oceans

Warm winter day by the sea
Surfing among the waves
Salty bubbles frothing
Refreshing renewing
How bloody lucky we are
Our present so serene
Waves lapping our luxury.
Thoughts turn to others
Their ocean a long road
Towards a new future
Escaping a doubtful past
Knowing how lucky we are
Not envious but a dream
For family free from want.

Time is ...

Time for tolerance
Time for peace
Time to offer a hand
Time to be aware
Time for one world
Time all people
Time all genders
Time all colours
Time all ages
Time our past made
Time for our future!

Microsoft Clip Art

Status update

Too long since a post,
My status unknown,
Though King Wiki might know,
If he were allowed to venture
As a fun-loving creature,
Like you, me and a gatepost
Hoping the underdog's
Bark is not silenced.
Would you really care
If a dog peed on my leg,
Or a dog dug up a bone
That was really your own?

Water gliding

Two in a boat did glide
On a watery ride
Where many years ago
Another canoe did go
Not of manmade material
But of cover from the trees
The paddle dark and serene
Gliding so as not to be seen
Arm above his head, spear
Flies through a fish without fear
Food enough for those who wait
Then to sleep as sun abates.

    – ***Reflection at Lake Boreen.***

Pray tell

Wonder why
People die
Why we care
More when
Children taken
Before time
When life ready
To challenge
Want answers
But taken sooner
Than reason permits
Questions painful
Answers curiosity
Query gods to know
Why no response comes
Despite despair
As perfectly good prayers
Remain unanswered.

Yuletide time

Waves of wishes
Flood the earth
Ripples of love
Become tides
Of time feeling
For those we love
With us now
In body today
Or yesterday
Maybe always
As Christmas
Shines a light
On memories
And fleeting
Missed souls
Making happiness
Eternal wrapping
Our hearts.

Scenario

Headline act,
Boat arrives unknown.
People on board from Somewhere,
Searching, seeking peace for
Loved ones and country maybe,
Or just what's needed to live.
Ahh! Landed at a wharf called Bulimba,
Dead of night unseen,
Rudderless,
Just a little obscene,
Couple copulating on the wharf,
Maybe for the country and local Member.
The seekers land and ask asylum,
But the people they are seeking
Are actually running that asylum!

Poll of omens

Felt an election coming on
Omens coming loud and strong
Shock for incumbents
Cheers for challengers
Volatility called the media
In need of some remedial
But not just a warning bell
More like a poll from hell
For some others heaven
Souls to be searched
A new era is birthed
Checkmate your knight
As queen wins the night.

– *Queensland, February 2015.*

For Australia's Day

Don't overdo the Aussie bit,
Don't try to be the biggest hit,
Enjoy the party, don't be a slob,
Don't let 'em say you're not worth two bob,
Enjoy yourself without being a wreck,
If an impulse comes just wait a sec;
Enjoy the day for a great south land,
From highest mountain to golden sand,
Spare a thought for those who were first
Long before Cook on the British purse
Married us to a kingdom far away
Over centuries becoming what we are today:
A nation, a people, showing respect
To self and to others as they would expect,
An example to nations of living together
Through storm, fire, all kinds of weather,
We're not perfect by any means
But still aiming to fulfil our dreams.

Badge marking Australia Day 1916 – National Museum of Australia, from a Lannon Harley colour photo.

What may be

Comes a time
When even a rhyme
Makes no sense
For recompense
Or what reward
Is untoward
To proffer
To make an offer
Or decline
As a sign
You're beyond
Singing a song
For sixpence
Or five cents
Or a holey dollar
What may follow
In time to reason
Whatever season
And so it goes
As life flows
Towards eternity
Whatever may be.

Murder on the nile express

There was a man called nile
Thought he had a charming smile
Many saw it as snide and smartin
More so over comments on Martin
Deriding people under threat
More than him we can bet.
None did there job he asserts
Except the would-be terrorist.
Maybe Fred Nile's had his time,
With due respect, has his mind
Gone towards a place seNILE
Or maybe he is a good example
To separate god and parliament.

- *On comments of a certain NSW parliamentarian on Martin Place siege December 2014.*

Arabian nights

Ally of the democratic world?
a young Saudi male whipped
50 times in a Jeddah square
Plus the same for 20 more weeks
... that all?
Oh, then 10 years in jail.
He insulted Islam on a blog!
Freedom's just another word;
So are justice, love, hate
In the name of prophets
Who espoused love;
Freedom to pray
Freedom to laugh
Freedom to reflect
Freedom to effect
Freedom to worship
Freedom to ignore.

Elegy in a country churchyard

(Apologies to Thomas Gray, "Elegy Written in a Country Churchyard", 1751)

It was morning when we gathered
In that country town of childhood
Seemingly familiar faces weathered
Names escape me, their recall is good.

Commemoration or celebration?
The church's 50 years have passed,
Many have been in adoration,
Others now have breathed their last.

This churchyard not like Gray's,
Though some cows head for home,
No tolling curfewing for the day,
Black and white, cream and rhone.

No rugged elms just gnarled gums,
Ironbark and wattle up the hill,
Shady in the setting sun
Against the sky an old windmill.

A surviving priest arrives to bless
All gathered, waiting silent within,
For their turn sins to confess,
Cursing drought their only sin.

My father recalled with others
For the role they played to build
This church in those struggling years
They prayed it was God's will.

Functions in backyards, on farms,
Raising money for a temple
Many themselves needing of alms

But being of such fine mettle.

Praying people, rain or peace,
Beseeching for better times
That nagging drought would cease
They might see better climes.

Trucks arrive near the rail station
Laden with the golden grain
Hope enough for the bank ration
Plus some for ample food again.

Around the time of Advent
They thank the Christian god
Though feeling all is spent
To even turn another sod.

After harvest celebration
Summer visit to the coast
Surf and sun, all sensation,
Before they start another quest.

Gray no doubt had an edifice
In quaint old Stoke Poges
About which to elegise
Simpler town here for the ages.

Church of Giles, a saintly
Holy Helper of the Camino,
Named for Immaculate Mary
This little church not long ago.

Gray lies always in his churchyard
But our church has no graves
Only memories of other times
When, pray, God had more sway.

Here a town below a hill
In the shadows of its own past
Claims a piece of history
As cars go by on the bypass.

Memories of time at school
Inkwell, copybook and pen
Good writing was the rule
In another time back then.

Few went further after that,
Boys went back to farms,
Girls helped mum or worked
And turned on all their charms.

No luxury or pride round here
Just hard work and sweaty days
Season by season, year by year,
Crops of wheat, oats and maize.

Milking their madding cows
Every morning and at night
Feeding crabby boars and sows
Tired and hungry by last light.

When old enough, off to dances
Swig of a bottle ridded shyness
Then went chasing some romance
Sometimes kiss and a caress.

Others who'd gone to high school
Came back home for holidays,
Knew a book but not a tool
And all the latest city craze.

Lonely boys and sweet girls
In the shadows of these elite
Dancing so cool around the halls

Always timing for the beat.

Hug 'fond breast' as 'parting soul'
After holidays returns to class
Leaving country friends to the role,
Being familiar makes them brash.

Old enough to borrow Dad's car
Now after dancing off to park
Fervent love under a star
Carried away they make a mark.

Next thing it's all surprise
Nervous down on bended knee
Sweet glistening in the eyes
Wonderful bride for all to see.

Soon children one, two, three
Growing up a choice to be made
Stay at home or on to degree,
So many options will be weighed.

A town that's so much of the past
Now stands around the church
Where two others also last
As people so different search.

Factory's long forgone cheese
And industry has all but ceased,
People go elsewhere for peace
With churches hardly ever used.

Store where we were the keeper
Now struggles to stay viable
Same with baker and the butcher
Big city now is too much rival.

THE EPITAPH

Remembered as a country boy
Or even a son of the Darling Downs,
Whatever, a mix of sad and joy
And family days in smaller towns.

Memories maybe of other days,
Rides in trucks and on the farms,
Playing rugby and social ways,
His adventures setting off alarms.

War and peace, work and play,
Together love creates two sons,
Writing, winding down his days,
Farewell to the beating drums.

Darling Downs scene – photo Helen Nolan.

Some other writings:

Reflections on newspapers

ALL this talk in recent times of the demise of the newspaper as we know it stirred memories of a different time.

A time when the sub-editors were the font of all knowledge on grammar, spelling, style and local history and geography … and everything else; a time when editors, not accountants, ran newspapers; a time when molten lead was used to make columns of type; a time when 'cut and paste' meant that, and spikes were sharp; when the most dogmatic of all reporters, a little Pommie in Toowoomba, told me not to be dogmatic when I challenged him, but then he did stir up visiting PM Malcolm Fraser who went to the editor's office to complain;

It was a time when the local Magistrate's Court daily sitting might last only a couple of hours after which our court reporter would go off to the pub with the Magistrate till mid-afternoon, then walk unsteadily back across the road to his desk and type his reports without ever a mistake.

Answering the newsroom phone one day I had the hospital medical chief – an eccentric chap – on the line inviting me up to 'see something'; when I arrived we walked down through the grounds to a nondescript, unlabelled building; he opened the door theatrically and there on the floor was a body in a shroud which was partly burnt. I was to discover that a 'mental ward' escapee had got into the building, the morgue, and apparently opened a 'fridge' door, lit a match to find food, but saw a face instead and somehow pulled the corpse onto the floor in his shock, dropping the match and burning the shroud. Poor chap probably couldn't wait to get back to his ward.

In the 'comp room' there was a special skill in working with lead type. One comp, another Pom, was so slick at working the lead galleys and filling up columns on the weekly free throw-away paper he nearly put it to bed with the Bishop's obituary – it wasn't complete; the Bishop was still alive. They filled that rag with anything as it was used mainly for supermarket ads carried over from the daily paper. The weekly was kept alive to keep out any opposition.

Off to Sydney to sub on the august *Herald;* I'd made it to Broadway (the area of Sydney where the paper was based then). It was an experience for a boy from the bush, especially on a Friday night seeing around 200 pages, two to a 'stone', on trolleys in a cavernous room. Somehow thousands and thousands of copies of the huge Saturday paper – mostly classifieds – came off the press in order.

In those days the Fairfax empire was still family and going well, with staff everywhere, executive titles everywhere. The Editor was 'God', but there were lots of other 'editors' wandering around with bits of paper and trying to look busy – at least up to lunch. One roundsman avoided typing out his stories by calling up a copytaker, who was only in the next room, and dictating his stories.

To Lismore as chief-sub, where my passion for balance got me into trouble. Fraser had delivered his Liberal policy speech one night in Sydney and got Page 1 coverage; the next night Bill Hayden did the Labor launch in Brisbane and Doug Anthony did the Country Party thing at Tweed Heads. I gave Hayden Page 1 and gave Anthony a Page 1 pointer to Page 2, which after all was exclusively local news and he *was* the local Member. His in-laws had interests in the paper in nearby Murwillumbah. Well, next day *it* hit the fan as to why the local boy wasn't on Page 1. He coincidentally visited as well and colleague John Stubbs, who had been a former national reporter and Labor media advisor, interviewed him.

In Kingaroy, where I became editor, I had a similar experience when I was questioned over giving a run to a couple of statements from the Labor candidate – who would always be flat out making double figures in a percentage share of the vote. The boss suggested that the share of coverage should match the anticipated share of the vote. Of course the long-term local member was Joh (later Sir) Bjelke-Petersen. Cold type (type on adhesive-backed paper rather than lead) was just coming in and one compositor thought that made it easy – if you didn't watch him, he would just slice off anything left over at the end of a column.

We had a major scoop with a much-anticipated report of a government inquiry into the Peanut Board. Trouble was it would be presented to

Parliament at 10 am on a Wednesday, the same time as our weekly newspaper was to come out. I made some discreet inquiries and got a call to say a copy of the report was on the daily plane from Brisbane; I picked it up and spent most of the night writing enough articles to fill the first three pages next morning – despite some legal reservations.

After I went to the 'dark side', with government, I still was lucky enough to deal with a great variety of interesting journos, both 'old school' and 'new school'. They were competitive, demanding and sometimes aggressive, but there was nothing like the contracted news cycle of today. It is difficult to forget 'Shaggers' (his rugby nickname) from *The Sun*, who would regularly call on a Friday afternoon when it was obvious he'd had a long liquid lunch; his tirade would start off something like: "What are you Tory bastards doing about the starving kids at … "

When I saw the *Cunnamulla Watchman* (actually *Warrego Watchman*) featured recently on the ABC *Australian Story* I realised how much the newspaper world has changed, but how much it is still the same – maybe with a different spirit and culture, without the individuality, yet with the same reason for being? As Columbus might have said: "There is a whole new world out there".

- *An edited version appeared in The Courier-Mail, Brisbane, on 18 January 2014 in 'Have Your Say'.*
- *PHOTO: Toowoomba's former Court House (now in private use) – Murray Views photo from Toowoomba Regional Council local history library.*

An amazing month on the other side

What a way to gain a taste of Europe in a month, alternating between frenetic cities and calmer rural areas with their contrasting pace and lifestyles.

After an overnight stopover in Dubai and a busy couple of days in London, the south-west of Ireland seemed in a different world, with Paris a mind-blowing follow-up for three days, before a needed recovery period in the south-west of France – apart from the stress of left-hand driving – and then by train to Barcelona to be greeted by a storm, out of there for a walking tour in the north on the Costa Brava, a mad day back in Barcelona, before a restive train trip back to London, and quiet days in the contrasting Scottish cities of Edinburgh and Glasgow, a wet stopover in the lovely Lakes District of England before a few wrap-up days in London and the long, sapping trek home.

People ask: what was the highlight? For a 60-year-old on his first trip to the UK and Europe – with the invaluable guidance of Caroline – every day was a highlight, most days with more than one. The Sagrada Familia in Barcelona, though, is something that seems out of this world. Work began on this imposing religious edifice in the 1880s and is still going on, with hundreds of tourists streaming among giant skeletons of scaffolding and cranes, even by lift and stairs up its symbolic towers.

Back to the beginning – almost: Dubai. It is worth a stopover but not memorable enough and too ostentatious for a holiday or even a return. While there are some striking modern towers, a highlight was below the surface: an underground museum graphically portraying the area's history. Great city if you want to shop till you drop, or till your card runs out.

In to London to be a greeted in a relatively relaxed atmosphere considering the recent terrorism episode (2005). Even on the train from Heathrow to Kings Cross, there appeared to be little tension. A Sunday afternoon walk around the city and across the Thames followed to find an oyster festival and then a pub roast dinner of course. Next day it was off to the colourful Portobello Road markets, Nottage Hill, Kensington Gardens past the Princess Diana Memorial, with a visit to Harrods and an extravagant treat of oysters and champagne. Even at the Changing of the Guard security was unobtrusive, but obvious. Trafalgar Square was crowded with people outnumbering the pigeons. We found an eccentric restaurant, Sarastro, in Covent Garden decorated with a stunning variety of stage props and art on the toilet walls that was interesting to say the least. It was a thrill that night to attend the long-running, acclaimed *Les Miserables* at the Queens Theatre.

Next day, despite a fretful train trip to Heathrow because of signal problems, it was off to Ireland with a casual welcome from customs and car hire officials at Shannon Airport. First stop Bunratty Castle, one of many to impress, and a lunch of a Guinness and a toasted salmon sandwich. An impressive old church built beside the ruins of an even older church at Buttevant was the arranged venue to meet family-tree connection Geoff O'Donoghue. He and family members gave a warm welcome and accommodation for two nights. Apart from meeting locals at Geoff's Pub at Castlemagner, a local highlight is the Kantirk Castle built in 1625.

It was not far from there to Killarney and on to the spectacular Ring of Kerry with a night spent in an old abbey at picturesque Sneem. Driving a car is challenging enough on the winding, narrow roads, but how much more so for the dozens of buses on the route. At Portmagee it was into a not-large boat for a half-hour ride out to the majestic Skellig Michael, a pair of rock islands on the edge of the Atlantic, one of which has a 1400-year-old monastery standing on its 182 metre peak *(pictured)*. It was a tough and nervous climb but worth it. Bernard Shaw visited in 1910 and commented: "An incredible, impossible, mad place. I tell you the thing does not belong to any world that you and I have lived and worked in; it is part of our dream world." One can only agree.

After a visit to another family connection at Dromoleague, south of Cork, a long drive to Dublin followed with a little Irish luck allowing discovery of Trinity College, Ireland's oldest university founded 1592, and pre-booked lodgings. Unfortunately, the accommodation was not on the historic campus itself but over the road in a more recently built plain concrete "jail". Trinity College boasts the Book of Kells, which is the centrepiece of an exhibition attracting 500,000 visitors a year. Written around the year 800 AD, the Book of Kells contains a richly decorated copy of the four gospels in a Latin text based on the Vulgate edition (completed by St Jerome in 384 AD). I needed to tell you that.

Apart from many great bars and shopping in a city centre based on the River Liffey, Dublin has many wonderful buildings apart from Trinity such as Dublin Castle. The Guinness Storehouse is naturally a popular spot for tourists: More than three million have visited its multi-floor information centre topped by the modern Gravity Bar with its near 360-degree views of Dublin. Of course there is a huge merchandise shop with a massive range of signature products.

From Dublin to Paris: no two cities are alike and these certainly are not. Dublin was relaxing compared with the frenzy and flamboyance of the French capital. A crowded bus trip from the airport was soon forgotten when it terminated at the grand Opera National de Paris building, though we had a passing look at the Stade de France on the way. And for shoppers, opposite the Opera is Galeries Lafayette, a shopping centre with a simply amazing interior dome and exquisitely decorated windows. Not far away is the clothing store of French rugby legend Serge Blanco, Quinze (that is, 15), where I bought an over-priced shirt.

Of course, in Paris one had to climb – by lift – the Eiffel Tower and also visit the *Louvre* with its rare and priceless works of art; the *Mona Lisa* seeming to attract the most attention (no sign of the Da Vinci code and all that). Thought they both have magnificent statues, memorials, palaces and other grand structures London has a degree of subtlety compared with the way Paris struts its history and culture. Gastronomically, Paris of course has much to offer but I would not recommend the tripe sausage (I forced half down while a local at a nearby table had no trouble. Mind you, staff at the traditional, cute Les Noces de Jeanette had warned me).

A pleasant way to escape the narrow noisy lanes, the scooters and dogs of Paris and see the country side was the train to the South-West town of Perigueux where we picked up a hire car and learnt very quickly to drive on the wrong side of the road. Driving into our destination, Brantonne, was a delight, like going back to another age. Most of the town lies on an island in the Dordogne River and looks like it would have centuries ago except for the cars – and ATMs. On the opposite river bank is an ancient abbey and convent, behind which are cliffs with large caves and overhangs housing shops and other premises. The hotel, Les Freres Charbonnel provided excellent accommodation and had a fine, apparently popular restaurant. Market Day was a highlight with a great range of food, including of course *foie gras*, herbs and spices, and clothing (Caroline tried on jeans in a temporary 'changeroom'). Nearby at Grotte de Villars we visited fascinating ancient limestone caves featuring crystal-like stalagmites and stalactites and paintings from another age.

As my left-hand driving improved, in the country where Australian writer Mary Moody spends some of her time, we aimed to stop for dinner and the night – not open, though it is Saturday. So on to Cahors, a town of only 20,000 with a fascinating 12th century tower bridge in remarkable condition. Next day, the 400,000-strong Toulouse was daunting for a novice left-hand driver, but we made it to the drop-off at the station and a train for Barcelona.

Arrival in Barcelona on a dark and stormy night was impending, but the taxi made the hotel at reasonable cost. Check-in was followed by a scary half-hour in a lift jammed by a blackout. Next morning was a hectic, mind-blowing bus tour of only some of the city highlights including the Gothic Quarter, the inspiring Cathedral (different from Sagrada Familia but also awesome), the Port, Olympic village and stadium, and Poble Espanyol (Spanish Village). In the afternoon it was off by train to Flaca near Girona and the Costa Brava in the north for a six-day walking tour.

The tour was exceptional value, though one wondered why the taxi driver was smiling when she dropped us off in the countryside. Did she wonder why we were doing it? The instructions soon had us on the right track – we hoped. The ambling trek through the quiet roads and tracks was relaxing apart from the odd barking dog and strong farm smell. The day was to end with a steep climb, but the reward was accommodation for the night in a

14th century castle, Castell d'Empordà (The Mediterranean coast and adjacent inland hills north of Barcelona are known as The Empordà). The original has been restored and added to by the Dutch owners, but it is an idyllic, dreamlike experience capped by a wonderful restaurant with slick service and superb meals. The Headwaters package included two nights here, with a "voluntary" walk locally on the "rest day", and next day we were off on a long walk towards the coast via the well-preserved ruins of an Iberian settlement in the hills at Puig Sant Andreu, dating as far back as the 6th century BC. After 15km including a large traditional lunch we made another historic town, Pals, but the hill to our two-night stop at Begur was too daunting: with the help of an English-speaking local we managed to get a taxi to the Hotel Rosa which is tucked in a closely settled enclave below the domineering Castell de Begur. After a sumptuous dinner, we made up for missing the last section of the day's walk with a winding, staggering climb to the top of the *castell* to be rewarded with a night view of the coastline, part of the famous Costa Brava *(pictured).*

Next day a long, steep downhill walk led to the beach of Sa Riera. The water was lovely and the weather warm and clear but, maybe because it was after the busy season (just), the showers were not operating and only one mobile toilet was available. The walk around the cliffs and the beachside café made up for the shortcomings.

Next day, past the statue commemorating legendary flamenco dancer Carmen Amaya, who was born and died here, the route follows the beautiful coastline to San Sebastian and Palafrugell. The nude photo session we came across was not on the notes. Some tough uphill and downhill sections were made easier by the beauty of the coves and the clear blue Mediterranean, plus the thought of lunch overlooking the sea at

San Sebastian – alas, it was closed, despite being a Saturday. It was on to the sedate Llfranc for a beachside lunch, and then another hour-long walk to finish at the same resort where we began, Hotel Garbi at Callela de Palafrugell. After a recovery night and a debrief, it was back to Barcelona on a quite Sunday train and the visit to Sagrada Familia; afterwards, coffee nearby and another view. At night a relaxing dinner with hundreds of passers-by and buskers on the magic La Rambla, a long mall closed to private traffic; Barcelona buzzing on a balmy Sunday evening in October.

Next day Caroline flew out to Denmark to visit her son Mark on Rotary exchange there; after a needed quiet time a visit to a couple of museum including Picasso's seemed a good idea – sorry, not open on Monday. I caught an overnight train to Paris before catching a lunchtime high-speed Eurostar across the French countryside and under the Channel to London. Overnight in London and then I was sitting back in another train: a comfortable way to see some of England and Scotland in a hurry, leaving Kings Cross in London for Edinburgh via Durham, Newcastle and York. On a mostly fine day, the English countryside was a treat, sipping tea and munching shortbread from the trolley in the train. Near the end of the journey, spectacular coastal views and a nuclear power station featured. Though I had seen it in still and moving pictures, I was still taken aback by the sheer, over-bearing presence that Edinburgh Castle has over the city around it. The city itself was bustling with hundreds of tourists, though after peak season; the Castle remains the attraction with workers there still dismantling the grandstands from the annual Tattoo. A nearby small Writers Museum featured Scott, Burns and Stevenson. Near the town centre a bagpipe busker played in the shadows of a huge monument to Sir Walter Scott and a smaller one for Livingstone – I presume. Next morning a tour inside the Castle, including the Scottish War Museum and War Memorial provided some inspiring moments.

A short train trip to Glasgow was again a scenic joyride, before arrival in a city that was, against expectations, clean and welcoming: apparently this famous city is fighting back after challenging setbacks following the demise of coalmining and shipbuilding, with a resulting serious decline in population. With another family-tree connection, Mary, as a guide, nearby Loch Lomond was a special, peaceful setting and the city itself has some spectacular buildings such as the Peoples Palace (museum) fronted by a unique Empire Fountain, an imposing city square, and a majestic precinct which includes an inspiring Glasgow University and Art Gallery (closed for refurbishment).

From Glasgow a Virgin train took me to the Lakes District, featuring beautiful Lake Windermere, for a stay at one of innumerable B&Bs. The area has the homes of William Wordsworth at Rydal Mount and Dove Cottage – originally a pub built in the 16th century – and the adjacent Wordsworth Museum. The only disappointment was the lack of recognition for his talented and devoted sister, Dorothy. However, a guided tour of the Cottage was intimate and educational. Because of rail works, a crowded and uncomfortable bus ride was necessary before eventually catching a Virgin train again at Preston; and back to London. By the way, train travel, both regionally and the undergrounds in London, Paris and Barcelona, are mostly efficient and easy to use.

Next day, time to catch up on a few sites: the 'famous' Elephant Castle pub was a major disappointment, but a visit to the nearby Imperial War Museum was sobering – particularly so the Holocaust Exhibition (children under 14 not allowed for reasons that become apparent) – and a tube ride to Trafalgar Square for lunch before a compulsory walk down the Mall for a visit to Buckingham Palace; but did not go in and missed HRH. The morning brought another fine day – as most had been – and return of Caroline from Denmark. Fine weather gave us a great chance to "ride" the London Eye before forecast wet weather arrived. And a super experience it was: a slow, calm ride in a capsule on a giant wheel offering expansive views of this special city.

At night back at Sarastro *(pictured)*, in Covent Garden you may recall, for Caroline's birthday celebration: romantic atmosphere, singers with violin and cello accompaniment, followed by two versatile divas, fine wine and sumptuous menu (with 'in-laws' Trudy and Andy). In the morning, last day – rest? No way: off for a Thames cruise to Canary Wharf, a new business centre near where the 2012 Games will be, and a monorail trip back to Tubeland. Then to Heathrow and home.

Reflections: While Barcelona and its Sagrada Familia were something special, so was everywhere else, but not so surprising. That is to say, Britain, Ireland and France maybe were places I was used to through reading, pictures, television, whatever, and were not such a novelty, though so wonderful and spectacular with a few exceptions. Also, customer service at most places was often disappointing in the UK and Europe. Generally, waiters, air stewards, counter staff and others seem aloof, too formal and serious, even unfriendly – maybe it is just a reaction to Australian familiarity or a language issue in France and Spain (I wonder if the arranged and confirmed birthday cake for Caroline is still in the Emirates galley). Certainly, on return to Brisbane airport the Customs people were both efficient and friendly: "Gday Mate!"

- *Edited version of an article written after the trip in 2005.*

Family's link ends after 100 years

A 100-year link with Irongate has been broken with the sale of the last Mahoney property in the district.

'Fairview' is being sold by Noel and Marie Mahoney, who are retiring to live in Pittsworth.

Noel's grandparents, Patrick and Johanna Mahoney (*pictured*), first bought a property at Irongate in 1913 called 'Oakview', later moved across the road in to a new home, retaining the name 'Oakview', which they moved to in 1929. It became available with the breaking up of St Helens Station.

Patrick was born in 1878 at Warra, west of Dalby, his parents later moving to Warwick. They moved to Acacia Creek in New South Wales so he left home at 13 to become a stableboy at Glengallan Station north of Warwick. Legend has it that he was a boxer and cricketer of note.

Johanna was a teacher at Sugarloaf in northern New South Wales before joining the staff of Stanthorpe Convent. She and Patrick were married in in 1903 at St Joseph's Catholic Church in Stanthorpe and moved to Pittsworth in 1908. He worked at any jobs available and, with carpentry skill, erected the paling fence around St Stephens Catholic Church. He was also skilled in butchering and owned the local slaughter yards for a period.

After looking at several possibilities, they bought their first Irongate property in 1912. Their oldest son, Jeremiah (known as Joe), took up 'Fairview', next door to 'Oakview', in 1937 following his marriage to Gretta Daly.

Their other children were Elizabeth (known as Beth, born 1906), Mary Eileen (known as Eileen, 1909), Kathleen (1910), Dorothy (1915), John (known as Jack, 1917), Vincent (1919) and Ivan (1923).

Apart from Joe, who was a shire councillor for 22 years, two other sons stayed in the area – Vince farming on another property not far from where he had grown up and Ivan farmed 'Oakview' after his parents retired in 1954. Vince married a local school teacher, Esme Kiorgaard, and Ivan a music teacher, Kathleen Sullivan, whose parents farmed 'Bantry' in the Pittsworth area.

Three daughters remained in the Pittsworth district – Beth married Bill Naumann and they farmed at Springside; Dorothy and her husband, Malachy (Mally) Sullivan farmed at Spring Vale; and Kathleen and husband Ken White had a mixed grocery, fuel and grain business at Mount Tyson. Eileen married a postal officer and they lived in Brisbane while Jack married Mary Gleeson and they farmed at Irvingdale near Dalby.

Patrick and Johanna lived in a newly built home on Vince and Esme's property after leaving 'Oakview' in 1954 and later lived with Bill and Beth at Springside. Patrick died in 1962 and Johanna in 1973, a year after moving to Toowoomba with Bill and Beth.

Dorothy, now 98, is the sole surviving member of the family and lives at Beauaraba Lodge in Pittsworth.

Many descendants of Patrick and Johanna Mahoney, whose graves are at Pittsworth Cemetery, live in the Pittsworth area or else more broadly on the Darling Downs.

Recently, about 70 descendants and family attended a reunion at 'Fairview' to mark the 100 years and the impending breaking of the family link with the Irongate district.

- *About my mother's family – Information from* **Mahoney-Hannon Family Tree** *by Denise Quinn and Kaye O'Connell. Article published in* **The Pittsworth Sentinel** *13 November 2013. Noel Mahoney passed away on 14 December 2014, aged 75 year. Dorothy will be 100 on 29 March 2015. The area referred to is near Toowoomba in Queensland.*

Churches big and small

When I visited the *Sagrada Familia* in Barcelona I could not help but think of a small country church back in Australia.

A few years later when I walked the historic Camino in the same country small churches along the way stirred the same memory, though they were much older and their design and construction very much a contrast. Mostly they were stone compared with the chamfer on brick of the church back home.

The church in my memory is Mary Immaculate (opened 1958) in my home town of Mount Tyson. It is a special Catholic church, not because I am particularly religious, but more because of the prominent role my father had in raising the funds to build it. He died before it was built, but would have been proud indeed that what he started had come to fruition – and he would have been quick to acknowledge the efforts of others.

Ken White had died suddenly at home on 25 July 1956 aged 44, leaving his wife, Kath (see previous story), and six children. Apart from working in a business partnership which served the district as a general store, post office and grain and fuel agency, he also found time to be involved in the church fund-raising, the town progress association, the school committee and the church's Hibernian Society.

As his obituary in the Toowoomba-based regional newspaper reported, "The long cortege to the cemetery at Toowoomba was a striking tribute to

Rose Cottage, the oldest slab hut in Australia, at Wilberforce near Windsor NSW – Heritage Council NSW photo.

one of Mt Tyson's most prominent residents." He was also described as a "well-known and highly respected resident of Mt Tyson".

James Kennedy (known as Ken) White was born at Jondaryan near Toowoomba on 1 December 1911, the fourth and youngest child of James and Ethel (nee Baldock).

James senior had been born a seventh child at Jondaryan in 1871 after his parents came from Ireland, his father Patrick having married Mary Kennedy in County Kilkenny in 1858. He went to school at Jondaryan State School and later worked at the iconic Jondaryan Woolshed, records listing him as "stable boy, shed hand, generally useful, horse breaker, horse driver, drover and shearer." After leaving the woolshed he worked extensively with horses and was a carrier, timber dealer and building contractor as well as owning land in the area.

James married Ethel Margaret (known as Margaret) Baldock at St Mark's Catholic Church, Jondaryan, in 1901. She was born at Westbrook near Toowoomba in 1879, the first daughter of William and Agatha (nee Fogarty).

A timber slab hut built in 1811 by Agatha's great-great-grandfather, Thomas Rose, and son Joshua still stands at the Australian Historical Village at Wilberforce, New South Wales (It is the oldest timber slab dwelling in Australia, the village website states.) Thomas and his wife Jane, with four of their seven children, were among the first free settlers to arrive in NSW on the *Bellona* on 16 January 1793.

William Baldock was born in 1847 at Camberwell in NSW, the eighth child of Thomas and Hannah (nee Lusted) who had arrived in Australia on the *Prince Regent* in 1839. Agatha was the daughter of John and Margaret Fogarty (nee Kelly).

William and Agatha married at Wallabadah near Tamworth NSW in 1873 where William had a carrying business. A baby son had died when they moved to Westbrook in 1878 and lived on several properties where William worked as a carrier and farmer before a career change led them to move to Jondaryan to take over the Railway Hotel in 1889. They had four more children though twins had died soon after premature birth.

Ironically, a son Clarence was also involved in church fund-raising; he went to Chinchilla in 1899 and helped raise money for a Catholic Church there. He sang a duo at a fund-raising concert and next day was riding a horse called All's Luck when killed in a 'shocking accident'. It is said that Agatha had never got over her son's death when she passed away in 1902.

Margaret, their first daughter, had gone to school at Athol near Westbrook before the family moved to Jondaryan, attending the local school before finishing her education at St Saviour's in Toowoomba. Margaret was a talented pianist and taught music and played for many functions throughout the district. Following her marriage she and James lived on the family farm, known as "Kenmore."

Husband James died in 1934 in Tara, near Dalby, after what was described as a massive heart attack – the same cause as son Ken's death. James' work meant he was often away from home and several years earlier Margaret had moved to Toowoomba. She died two years after her youngest son in 1958.

They had three other children before Ken: Nicholas (Alan), who became a police inspector; Clarence, factory manager/shopkeeper; and Eileen (who married Arthur McNally; they became partners in the Mt Tyson business). Eileen was the last surviving member of the family when she passed away in 1988.

> −*Information supplied by my sister, Denise, a family historian.*
>
> −*PHOTO: My father and his mother at the piano.*

Time of learning and adventures

School's in ... vividly I recall the grey plywood box that was a loudspeaker sitting at the top of the stair belting out *God Save the Queen* as we marched into school under the watchful eye of a severe looking head teacher and other staff

Into class and copybooks, ink and pens with bent nibs; scratchy slates and blackboards, with a teacher's writing efforts often producing that piercing scratch that makes your nerves quiver; which also reminds me of the dentist, a government bloke that used to come and set up his stuff on the school veranda, with a painful drill that he operated via a foot pedal.

I don't remember the incident well, but there is a family story that I kicked my teacher in the shins on the first day.

When I was older I used to wag school and spend the day behind the sheds at the back of our store, probably having the odd fag. In later years I realised there was an underground store of fuel nearby.

A cigarette caused a problem for the head-teacher once. He (I suppose they were always male in those days) was disciplining me about something out in the playground and absent-mindedly put a cigarette butt – still alight – in his pocket, burning a hole.

Milk was supposed to be good for us, but I wonder how good the free government milk was that the mailman delivered and left under the jacaranda in front of the post office, often left for some time to be warmed by the sun. I recall that the mailman was the same Pittsworth bloke who used to come and empty the "dunny" drums in the middle of the night.

At least ice cream was kept cool in transport in tall green insulated containers with 'hot ice'. That was what we had on occasions such as break-up days – after the egg and lettuce and ham sandwiches of course. And break-up days were something special: Biggles and cowboy books for prizes. Races where everyone was a winner – I think, since I was among the slowest but managed a few banners.

But the big sports of what we then saw as being of Olympian proportions were at Rossvale. I have driven past since and find it difficult to identify even vaguely where they were in what now is just a bush area. There, kids from all the district schools did three-legged and sack races, tunnel and leader ball, march-pasts. By far the largest school in the district, Mount Tyson was divided into three teams.

Our own sports fields were hardly "Fields of Dreams", particularly when we mostly played barefoot. The school playground was hard with tufts of tough grass, as I recall. The field beyond was used for the horses of those who rode to school, and occasional cricket and football.

In senior years we donned the "whites" for cricket, playing as far afield as Quinalow or somewhere like that. Our cultural development was not forgotten – folk-dancing on the parade area or under the school with a bit of smart footwork needed to get next to the girl you fancied that day – though usually too shy to do much about it.

Mount Tyson Cheese Factory – Queensland State Archives photo.

The local hall was also an important focal point for the school and the rest of the community. There were regular fancy-dress balls where I once went as a jockey (gear borrowed from the local racing family, Buckley's at Purrawunda), which wasn't too bad, but the Little Boy Blue costume another year can't have done much for my macho image.

The hall was also used for school fund-raising events and all sorts of activities such as card nights, Mass for the Catholics and the QCWA. As with other venues for Mass, the supposed anonymity of Confession would be lost, as the cheerful priest would ask after parents and other family members. While Mount Tyson had no hotel, the Aubigny pub was not too far away. Many a double sars or cherry cheer – with chips –- was had there. Once we had to stay the night because Ziebell's gully came up after a downpour and stranded us.

Those simple times meant riding a bike up to Barlow's farm to get a billy of milk each morning, climbing the back fence for fresh bread from the local baker (Hobdell's and later Cooks), going around the corner to Cocky Kowitz's for meat. Old Mister Hanna used to come from Toowoomba in his van and park in front of our home in Side Street, selling clothes and stuff such as Chesty Bond singlets and y-front undies.

School holidays were good times when I would help our store delivery driver on his run around the district, a chance to catch up with schoolmates. Often I got to stay at friends' farms, helping with the milking, riding horses, driving tractors – and maybe flirting with their sisters. Even around town there was plenty to do: playing around the cheese factory, the station, grain sheds, Kowitz's loquat tree, the quarry, the "mountains" around town (where our fathers had gone on "Dads Army" exercises during the War). After storms, we would build dams across the wide gutters beside the roadway.

Many of my childhood memories are of those "mountains" – just hills really. I recall climbing Mount Tyson itself, which then must have seemed as significant a feat for a child as Everest was for Hillary around the same time. There we played war and cowboy-and-indian games. A few years later I graduated to nearby Mount Wyangapinni, the highest "hill" on the Darling Downs, I was led to believe.

We were torn between two larger towns: attending school and other activities in both Oakey and Pittsworth, and occasionally Toowoomba. Of course out store and nearby home were in Pittsworth Shire and the school across the road in Jondaryan Shire. When the Queen toured after her Coronation, we were taken across as a group with little flags to stand beside the road waving and cheering as she was driven from Oakey Airport to Toowoomba.

Those innocent years were soon left behind. The war games of childhood became serious when my mate from Irongate, Murray Jim Fletcher, and I – along with 5000 other Australians – were to serve in Vietnam. Some years afterwards, Murray Jim died tragically and there is a tree near the school entrance to his memory. There are trees for others who did not return from other wars. Lest We Forget.

- *Photo from the Royal tour – Queensland State Library.*

- *Article written for Mount Tyson State school centenary celebrations 2004. The author was a student in the 1950s.*

From little things ...

AS THE song goes, 'from little things big things grow'.*

Early last year a group of University of Queensland (UQ) medical students went to Kavieng in PNG to gain field experience with support from a Rotary Club of Toowong, Brisbane, project.

They reported back to the club that the x-ray department at the hospital was in need of protective clothing for radiography staff and patients.

The Rotary Club responded, contacting Rotarian Ray Crompton at Wesley Hospital who sourced six protective vests which were being replaced. The next challenge: how to get the vests weighing in total around 20kg to Kavieng.

Inquiries revealed that Newcrest Mining operated in the Kavieng area, so the club made an inquiry to ask whether the company could get the vests to the hospital. No problem, Newcrest responded, and off the vests went to be gratefully received.

The Rotary Club thought, why not build on the positive vibes from Newcrest Mining, so made a submission for company support towards shipping a container of medical and educational equipment to Kavieng through the Rotary District Donations in Kind (DIK) program.

This also received a positive response with a donation of $5500, and a container was soon on its way to Kavieng, arriving last week for distribution of the donated items which range from school desks to hospital beds.

The container is safe at the local pub under the watchful eye of Kavieng Rotarian Leo Badcock.

The Rotary Club of Toowong and Rotary district always welcome corporate and community support for the DIK program.

The club is also boosting its annual medical student program which is run in conjunction with the University of Queensland.

Both projects are examples of where the corporate sector, the community and community service organisations such as Rotary can work together to make the world a better place.

(* Song 'From Little Things Big Things Grow' – P. Kelly/K. Carmody.)

- *This article was printed in The Courier-Mail, Brisbane, on 21 July 2012 in the 'Have Your Say' section. The author was proud to be a member of the club when this project was undertaken.*

- *BELOW: Toowong Rotarians loading a container bound for Kavieng.*

Apprentice who became a hero

IN late February 2015 Sunshine Coast war veteran and former helicopter pilot Jim Campbell attended the 50th anniversary reunion of 5 Battalion Royal Australian Regiment. He caught up with Tony White, who was the battalion's doctor when Campbell flew him in to treat wounded soldiers after a major mine incident during the Vietnam War. Campbell was awarded a DFC (Distinguished Flying Cross) for his action. Here is my story about Jim Campbell:

AFTER 49 years as a helicopter pilot which included his war service, negotiating the mountains of Papua New Guinea and chief pilot for an emergency and rescue service, retirement might seem like a time for gardening, caravanning or just putting the feet up.

Not for Jim Campbell, DFC. How about hiking the Kokoda Track and riding through Europe on a World War Two-vintage motorbike?

Campbell sees nothing of the celebrity in his remarkable life – always a non-smoker and non-drinker, his life story seems to have been always one of looking for 'other things' to do.

After completing junior (Year 10) he left school in 1953 aged 15 to join the Army and become a 'spanner', as members of RAEME (Royal Australian Electrical and Mechanical Engineers) corps are slanged.

He went on to be the first Army apprentice to become an Army pilot, but even more significantly the first Army pilot to be awarded a Distinguished Flying Cross since 1918.

In Vietnam on 21 February 1967, during Operation Renmark he responded to the mayhem caused by two explosions, flying a doctor in to a horrific scene in the Long Hai mountains in his Sioux A1-404 Bell 47 helicopter – an aircraft similar to the bubble-nose aircraft made famous in the MASH movie and TV series.

Jim Campbell (left) and the author at the Maroochydore War Memorial. – Photo Sunshine Coast Daily/APN.

An APC (Armoured Personnel Carrier) had been blown apart by a mine and medics and others rushing to render aid were hit by another mine, resulting in nine deaths with 22 other wounded – a shattering day for B Company, 5 RAR.

His award citation reads: "At great personal risk Captain Campbell flew a medical officer to the scene of the mine explosions, and landed in the minefield knowing full well that he and his helicopter could be destroyed by a mine explosion triggered by the helicopters skids or the down blast of the rotors. He chose to do this so that by quick evacuation the lives of the more seriously wounded might be saved.

"With complete disregard for his own safety, Captain Campbell landed time after time in the minefield in order to evacuate the wounded to another landing point from which it was considered safe for large Royal Australian Air Force helicopters to operate and thus remove the wounded to hospital.

"By his skill, fortitude and special efforts to lift out the wounded at all costs, Captain Campbell set an outstanding example as a soldier, as an Army Pilot and his actions reflect great credit on himself, his unit and Army Aviation."

He recalled later: "I felt it was part of my job and with little thought for the dangerous situation, I didn't hesitate to carry out the evacuations."

Campbell was serving as a mechanic with an infantry battalion in Malaya when his potential to be a helicopter pilot was noticed. He had already gained a fixed-wing licence in his own time and flying was a hobby.

His first posting as an Army pilot was with a United Nations unit in Irian Jaya (now West New Guinea). Before being posted to Vietnam in 1966 he trained as an instructor in the United States.

After Vietnam he served in Papua New Guinea and had another year in the US before resigning from the Army in 1979. In Papua New Guinea he had probably his most serious incident when, as an instructor he took over the controls of a helicopter for landing at the end of a training flight.

"We went into a spin and slammed into the ground ending upside down in a mass of twisted metal. I was uninjured, but badly shaken of course, and my fellow pilot was hospitalised," he said. "The cause had not been fully investigated when 18 months later a similar accident with the same type of aircraft happened near Amberley with fatal consequences for both aboard; an investigation found that anti-torque controls on the instructor's side had been put in the wrong way around. An engineer had apparently done the same with mine."

One of his last 'missions' with the Army was to fly the same Sioux Bell 47 he piloted in Vietnam from the Army Aviation Centre at Oakey near Toowoomba to the Australian War Memorial in Canberra for display.

Then he ended up in another pioneering role, becoming involved with establishing the Sunshine Coast Helicopter Rescue Service, believed to be Australia's longest running community-based, not-for-profit helicopter operation, as both founding chief pilot and CEO.

After retiring from flying in 2005 he took on two land-based adventures – he trekked the Kokoda Track in PNG made famous by heroic Australian Diggers in World War Two and then later, aged 73, he took a trip to the Ukraine to buy a vintage motorbike and ride across part of Europe.

"A group of 20 of us, mostly older males from a variety of backgrounds, arrived at a rundown workshop on a former Soviet airbase to collect the bikes," Campbell recalls. "They were Russian-built copies of a World War Two German Army BMW bike with sidecar. Mine actually has a Swastika imprint on the chassis.

"He has made a few long trips with the bike back at home, but mainly just rides it around the Sunshine Coast where he lives. For much of his life he was a passionate runner and in his younger days represented Queensland in the State Modern Pentathlon Team at the National Championships and won a Queensland orienteering championship.

At 75 he has given up running, but is a serious 'outrigger', rowing annually in the national titles. He and wife Chris enjoy regular snow-skiing trips in Australia and New Zealand as well as time with a son, two daughters and three grandchildren.

The author was a member of B Company 5 RAR on that day when Campbell won the DFC. He was in the last of the APCs (Tracks) taking the company up the Long Hai mountains when the first APC was hit by a mine. He recalls seeing the helicopter come in to the site, but only in recent years met Jim Campbell and realised he was that pilot. An edited version of this article appeared in **The Sunshine Coast Daily** *on 8 February 2015.*

PICTURED ABOVE: Dr Tony White (left) and Jim Campbell catch up at the 5 RAR reunion 2015 (The author and Tony are not related). Tony White has written a memoir, **Starlight - An Australian Doctor in Vietnam**, *available through starlightbook.com.au.*

Threescore years and ten! It is the Scriptural statute of limitations. After that, you owe no active duties; for you the strenuous life is over. You are a time-expired man, to use Kipling's military phrase: You have served your term, well or less well, and you are mustered out. – Mark Twain on his 70th birthday, 1905.

www.ingramcontent.com/pod-product-compliance
Lightning Source LLC
Chambersburg PA
CBHW032213040426
42449CB00005B/572